salmonpoetry

*Publishing Irish & International
Poetry Since 1981*

Rise

ELAINE FEENEY

Published in 2017 by
Salmon Poetry
Cliffs of Moher, County Clare, Ireland
Website: www.salmonpoetry.com
Email: info@salmonpoetry.com

Copyright © Elaine Feeney, 2017

ISBN 978-1-910669-83-9

All rights reserved. No part of this publication may be reproduced or transmitted in any form or by any means, electronic or mechanical, including photography, recording, or any information storage or retrieval system, without permission in writing from the publisher. The book is sold subject to the condition that it shall not, by way of trade or otherwise, be lent, resold or otherwise circulated without the publisher's prior consent in any form of binding or cover other than that in which it is published and without a similar condition, including this condition, being imposed on the subsequent purchaser.

COVER DESIGN: *Ray Glasheen*
TYPESETTING: *Siobhán Hutson*
Printed in Ireland by Sprint Print

*Salmon Poetry gratefully acknowledges the support of
The Arts Council / An Chomhairle Ealaíon*

for Ray

Acknowledgements

Acknowledgements to the following publications and editors in which some of these poems first appeared:

Stonecutter Journal (USA), *The Stinging Fly* (Ireland), *Oxford Poetry* (UK), *Pilgrimage Magazine* (USA), *New Writing Canada* (Canada), *The Wide Shore; A Journal of Global Women's Poetry* (USA), *Even the Daybreak: 35 Years of Salmon Poetry,* edited by Jessie Lendennie (Salmon Poetry, 2016), *The Rebel Papers* (Liberty Press, Ireland), *The Manchester Review* (UK), www.lizrochecompany.com, *Solas Nua* (USA), *The Bogman's Cannon* (Ireland), *Inkroci* (Italy), *The Lithuanian Spring Festival Almanac* and *Metai Magazine* (Lithuania).

"Wrongheaded" was commissioned by Liz Roche Company and premiered at Dublin Fringe Festival 2016. The stage show is produced and directed by Liz Roche and the film was directed by Mary Wycherely.

Contents

one

Before You Begin	11
Whisht	12
Hindering Hercules	14
In the Way	20
Antaeus	21
Today	25
Mother and Victoria Beckham	27
Jack	29
Egg	30
Venturia Inequalis	31
Journey West	32
Definition	40

two

The Harvest	42
History Lesson	44
Oak	50
on the nature of things	51
Alternative Truth	54
The Apology	55
The Management of Savage Chaos	56
Moderato	58
Getting the Priest for Roethke	60
Sinéad	61
There are Blooming Daffodils in December	63

three

Muse/ Amuse	65
I Am Not a Bog Queen or a Fig or a Pomegranate	66
In Montmartre with Degas	70
In the Garage with Degas	71
Pushing the Body	72
Your Belly is Full of Girl Child	73

and i hope that i don't fall in love with you	74
The **BANKSY** Girl	76
Player	79
The Marriage	80
Inventor	81
Dystopia	83

four

Wrongheaded	85
1 | Hand Fast |	85
2 | Liquescence |	85
3 | Vanishing |	86
4 | Kaleidoscope |	86
5 | Petrification or Condensation |	87
6 | St. Vitus' Dance |	88
7 | Petrified | Hardening | Permanent |	90
8 | Sucking Numb |	91
9 | Kick up a Dust |	92
10 | Enflame |	93
11 | Compliance |	93
12 | Honey Sac |	95
13 | Ice Cubes for the Ferry Trip and Purgatory |	95
14 | Gentlemen's Agreement Over Bouclé Coat |	96
15 | Baksheesh|	98
16 | Gavel-Kind |	100
17 | Tom Tiddler's Ground, Who Owns a Dead Woman? |	101

five

Rise	104
Notes and Acknowledgements of Influence	108
About the author	110

one

'Walk on air against your better judgement'

SEAMUS HEANEY

'Out of the ash I rise with my red hair.
And I eat men like air'

SYLVIA PLATH

Before You Begin

always remember
how the
wood pigeons sing

whooo   who hu hu

hear it throughout now
    throughout then

simmer some mandrake
with a pinch of orris root

do not allow to boil

sip

watch the rising chest

        then fall
a whisper
a promise

    stretch in the evening

Whisht

I dressed myself in the morning's hawkish cold,
lit by my neighbour's hand torch in the field over.

Early rise makes flickering reels on the curtain hem.
I painted on my face shadows in circles,

as he fed grazing silage to the cow on her knees,
full as a winter barrel of rainwater.

And me, willing hard to keep my powder dry,
or at the very least, today, hold my whisht.

Never quite sure of yesterday's mask or how
to retrace kohl lines onto thinning eyelids.

I'm shaky as the swarthy dark throws
strange-shapes on the goose-wing walls.

I consider leaving Mouth in the bottom drawer
for my heaving lips stray over damp furze

like vulture rats, the wild yellowish petals sucking
warmth from my eyes. There will be mistrust

on faces of people I hold company with, neighbour,
colleague, son, unless I pack away my pestering

sound box. I could hurl it over the High-Bridge
near the apple orchard in a hanging low-fog

so no more sound evaporates
from my cracked Picasso lips

proving I chased round this circle
so furiously wild as to leave no more

than an uncertain shadow, miles shy
of who I am, or once was.

Maybe I should just take to the bed,
like they did, keep watch on his cow,

down on her knees, belly thick and swelled.
Hold my whisht. Keep my powder dry.

Hindering Hercules

There's nothing holy about dying on a hospital ward.
There's nothing at all about it.
There's no worship or heroics in it.

In between a dim light and fifty-gram bleached bed sheets,
   I lie my body down.
My mother says my name over and over and over again in
   blind panic.
I think they should leave the windows open to let all the
   infection out.
Later they tell me there were no windows.
But in my splutterings and whisperings I think it
only humane to open the window.

My father always told me I was fine,

you look fine
you sound fine
you are fine
get up off the ground
you're fine

The dead don't bother me. I swerve to avoid the living.
   But the living dead make me sick.
Half of them dying from the madness of death and not
   death at all. Just madness.

I hate the living dead. They are nowhere.

Maybe you might help with the herding,
and sure it'll take that sick pasty look off your face,
is that infection back again?

Aren't you a lot weaker than your mother?
Jesus Christ above in heaven but I don't know where we got you from.
If you rubbed a bit of rouge onto your sour dough puss, you'd look
  a bit better.
You should try fight it, with your fists, fight it, you've no fight.
With your puss all pasty like a weak auld pucán.

I herd our animals in my mind, just like when my second
  son was crowning and he tore my muscles wide open.
All the animals are stamped F. I herd in my sleep. Royal blue F.

Schuch schuch schuch, I say, over and over and over again.

And I click my soft tongue to the back edge of my
  hard palate,
something mute and frothy to the click drum rhythm of
  oxygen.

Like a madwoman.

I count each animal in my care, their stumbly legs, their
  shiny rumps, the roan arches of their backs. Wool, leather
  and dusty mare-hair. I think of how fast a foal rises.
  And how we labour for so long.
Nurse for so long. Cradle for so long.

We've given her Magnesium and Steroids, some Adrenaline
  or Epinephrine, more Midazolam, Atropine. Jesus more fluids
  maybe. What the fuck is happening? Who is looking after her?
  Charge. Why did she let herself get into this state?

Code.

I think she's gone. Is she gone? She's gone.

You're not sick at all,
it's all those vitamins your mother is giving you,
drink up a mug of tea and put on a coat,

*I've a young horse for you to ride and sure
then we can have another mug of tea.
Your mother will ready us something.*

I can't move my legs. I can't feel them.
I've pissed myself again. I haven't waxed.

*Is that her husband? Jesus take him out. Get him to leave,
   somebody take him out.*

I scream in my head.

Why won't he leave?

They fire my silver watch at him. It's in sickening slo-mo.
I think of my health insurance policy, the mortgage, the
   banana in my son's lunch box and how rotten it must be
   getting, the passports all need renewing this May.

I grab a yellow necktie tight with my fist and my
   slaughterhouse eyes scream as this man shoves something
   down my throat. I mangle the yellow tie around his neck
   hard and his hands are shaking.

I think I could kill him.

He's lovely. I decide he's lovely and his aftershave is lovely.
   I lick his neck, I can get some air there.
Later that night or the next night or the night after that,
   I'm not sure, I ask my husband to read me a poem if I die.

I don't want them to come back around me like clucking
   hens with their yellow ties.
Hurting me. Hurting us. Squeezing the juice from my wrists.
Read me anything, out loud, but I've only Bukowski and
   Heaney and I'm not sure I want to die to the sound of
   either of them.

But they can be saying goodbye.

I want to hear the lines from Lordan's poem, I tell him
you're dead, do you hear me you're dead, you're dead do you hear me
   or something like that, something fucking angry or it'll
   be a blood sacrifice for nothing.

But I'm only fighting myself again, every inch of me, and my
   husband thinks it's too angry a poem to die to.
He draws the line at certain things.

And I respect him. Only him, he has a quiet way to silence
   me with his love. Fear on his face like a dirty winter's
   hangover in March.

And I love him. And he loves me and that is all, but I'm angry,
   and now I'm worried about the banana. We should be
   on a tracker mortgage. He'll never remember.

I think it would keep me alive, I tell him, *that kind of fight,
I'd stay alive just to spite the fuckers.*

To spite who? He asks me again.

To spite the fuckers, I'll stay alive to spite the fuckers.

I decide on Heaney, Bukowski's too scary for any end.
My last breaths will be nothing. Nothing. I'm not a tragedy,
   I'm not young or innocent.
I will find my way through any world I arrive at, I will
   bring my jarred-angry self to the table of dead souls
   and I will annoy them.
Best of all I'll just be dead. And I'll have no soul. That's what
   I'm wishing, but I hardly ever wish at all.
I never see the point.
I am not afraid of dying. Who the fuck am I to be afraid of dying,
   with the daily seas of infant blood? How do we explain
   that with language?

There are far worse things than death.

I am selfish and ready and tired, and like all the child-games of hide-and-seek I couldn't sit still for as a kid, flashbacks to every mother desperately hiding children in wardrobes, pits, under beds, under coats, under smugglers, in dinghys made from the thinnest of rubber, hiding in places not good for hiding. Behind curtains, in ghettos, feet sticking out. I can't play that game. It's not a game. It's a nightmare. I will jump out at the last minute, before you're supposed to, because the waiting is the worst. Thinking of those who tried to stop their infants crying out.

Sitting and waiting.

I will jump out before the end, because I'd rather take it hot and angry, ready, than whisper around, as the suspense turns ice-cold and be fucking afraid.

I can't bear suspense.

But perhaps you're willing death on yourself and anger will get us nowhere.

Is there anything you want to say to these people, any messages?

Yeah say go fuck yourselves, that is all.

Those I love, know my love.

I looked at Bukowski's marled face. Angry bastard. I have a fuchsia hoodie. My red Converse stick out from beside the bed, ready to be walked.
A plastic pen. The two poetry books. Heavy night cream. Vaseline. Roget and Gallio soap. Flowery, floral. Two Mother's

Day cards. Masks. Tubes. Bottled water. A kidney dish.
Phone charger. Mouth sponges. Suction tubes. Lots of
plastic bags with tubes. Worm tubes. Iodine. Nail clippers.

I'm so sorry, I say, over and over again. *I'm sorry*, I say. I'm
saying *sorry*. The wind takes it. The tea lady catches it.
Sorry, I say, and I take it to the stars over Newcastle and
to the doughy soft breasts opened out in front of me.
Sorry, I say to the children that came from me.
I whisper it to the moon and to the concrete walls,
to the plastic oxygen balloon, to my mother, *sorry,* I say
and the narrow grass-blades at the hospital entrance
grab it. *Sorry*, I say to my hate, *sorry* I say to the dark
and beautiful lark eyes of Heaney, just watching me.

Late spring red flowers grow from the grass blades and
I am not afraid.

Yet there are no words for the dying. Limp and flat,
no God's touch or water drop in sight so just read
to me I ask, and it's his choice,

'Show me,' I said to our companion, 'what
I have much coveted, your breast's mauve star.'
And she consented. Oh neither these verses
Nor my prudence, love, can heal your wounded stare.

Days later a young doctor with fusilli curls and a purple
face sits on the bed.
The imprint of my husband is proving.
He asks of my terror and tells me of his fright.
Then speaks of his mother. It's Mother's Day.

In the Way

The hospital takes
my words away

descriptions become
impossible

I cannot remember if
the yogurt left back

in the fridge is
hazelnut or chocolate

I'm not wearing knickers
because they were the last thing

I thought of when I began
saving my life

yet managing
to hide myself for
feeling in the way

again

like an old Christmas tree
or a three-wheeled van

relieved that machines
now speak for me
put me *on guard*
in the middle of the
resuscitation bed

where there's no
washing machine
or fridge
not even a curtain
to hide behind

to pretend this is

not happening.

Antaeus

I haven't walked my shoes farther than the length of our
    kitchen table in over
eight weeks. Today I begin again like a wheel free dinky
    car tumbling

down a tarmac'd hill. Sometimes I just do it as a tedious job,
    like working the till at Tesco,
or a wet summer packing warm hen eggs into cardboard
    cartons.

Or sometimes I do it to feel the turf a sort of solid earth
    underneath my feet-pads,
to stop me spiking up and then sparking off you,

and sometimes to give my bed-sored heels a break, the
    clear fluid slushes
and shoves hot up against blistered skin like a bloated
    surgical glove,

crowning like the last stroke of warm water from my
    dog's dead tongue,
now gone cold, and yesterday and today are nothing more
    than respiratory rates.

My wheezing annoys the fat robin that has taken squattage
    on the top of
our Christmas tree and reminds me of the soul of someone
    minding me.

You say,

Jesus Fucking Christ how can you be like this?

[How?]

You cried

[Light bulb word that was forgettable]

all day putting up that tree,
so really you're not minding yourself a'tall?
Do you want to be better?
We love you but you have to try.

[But I]

The next day you took me to the hospital across the city,
    I was shaking
and the next day they cancelled the operation,
    just like that,

just like you'd twist a little brittle fairy light bulb in a sort
    of flither,
and the tree would light up but die again, and the tree was
    tree-tree green.

I am leaving my things in there beside the red and black
    ladybirds,
they were all over the tree, *Lady Bird Xmas Year*,
    and ugly brown pinecones that looked threatening,

don't open them, they're a surprise, don't let a drop of rain
    ruin the surprise,
left here with all the glitzy presents and the food charred
    in the dirty oven.

[The fear]

It's just not fair on the kids
you crying all day
and when old poems about
anvils and tongs
came on the radio,
you were Queen Blubbery-
I thought the house ran
out of warmish water,
but you cried again.

I cried for the now disbelieving child grumped low in his corner,
kicking a flicking Xbox controller, a stranger in our kitchen,

for father a stone's throw away, light years to me ever
   touching the
mad matter inside his head and trying to rinse him out
   like you might do

with collected sandy pebbles in a red bucket out on
   Silver Strand
back Spiddal way, or maybe crying for this large woman
   night-boor

who haunts the front window walking the road like
   a telephone pole blown down sideways?

And that Christmas-crying made the shoes at the
   edge of the bed
look like two floating pairs. As if my-self and her-self,
   the crying-part and the light-part might step out together,

talk up to the robin and maybe get her down off
   the tree with a palm straight out and into the air.

Air, the saving of all ills.

I don't even know what to say,
I won't include our finished dialogue.

[The long road of recovery]

That two-way thing when my head aches, so I will myself
   to get out of
this house for an hour, reach farther than the coffin table,

attempt to walk in other shoes, see the world
   from above the

awkward contours of another foot, stronger calves in his
    ankle boots.

But strange shoes don't solve this same earth revolving like a
    disco ball,
making me dizzy, then balancing me cagey,

weeks-to-months-sheezy, bed-edgy, night-cappy, half-dreamy,
    half-sleepy.

Keep your feet on the ground girl, settle your body in this air.

Today

was a suicided priest book of condolences opened in my way
day. Everyone with an angle day. Today was a pus pimpled

teenage boy taking his money shot at my tits day, with a handful
of coins he owed me day, and said a fuck off or fucked me off

day, and the sky was a shy sky day letting nothing down only
rankle smog, it was ignoring my children day, until they

buckled day, so it fast became Victory Day but then to the mad
doubts of knowing they will never call me with a Pancor

Jackhammer in their hand day, because I'll be hanging the new
dappled red curtains or doing a draining the sink of sludge day,

don't interrupt me kind of day, and there are chores
more important than how you will sit yourself at the centre of

my day kind of day and demand me to pay you the kind of
unbalanced attention needed from a 50s cinema usher

or a posh train trek across Vienna or off a child psych day.
It was burnt sienna orange sweater day, and then worrying if

burnt sienna is a bit too poncey a west coast of Ireland kind of
day. Today was Sylvia Plath telling me she wanted to be a

carpenter or a doctor day. I agreed. I would love useful with my
hands kind of days. Save a life day. Save a wife day.

I wish it were a carve Sylvia&Ted weddingtopperday.
It could be a bake-cake day, if I could bake-cake with hands are

useful day, and I would ice a beige walnut and green kiwi cake
and give my husband decent head and not be shy about it

icing kind of day. And today was a traffic jam day and a
bluetooth conversation about memory with said husband day,

I don't know did I talk to him or to the soused air day.
Today was a church bell day and my hell was a mahogany

classroom window that wouldn't open day. Today was
my crying friend day and the bent pole of the trampoline

kind of day. It was a saturated day, a pouring rain day,
a Vivaldi dominated House of Pain Day.

Mother and Victoria Beckham

In the curved light
of coming night
the voices around
            the Formica table
filled the kitchen,
like when
I'd get the school bus home
and eat a bowl of stew,
chatting came in like
a lover knocking on
your bedroom window,
            or seed drills
shaken rhythmically
from hand memory.

Everything is more silent.
We've outgrown our mouths.

I want to dance wild,
a tribal mother wailing
at harsh spirits,
until a man holds his palm
to the small of my back
to stop my trunk snapping.

I want my children to wail
and learn how to get angry.

Here,
whispers go over and back
to the sound of television
like my window-wipers
pushing visibility out
the Curraghline.

She is dying.

Thump.

A heel of his
hand
to your chest,
to revive you,

*she is dying,
and I hate her dying,*

worms are
splayed open by
the spring spade.

Well now,

isn't it a year for deaths,

didn't Johnny,

Mother said,

lose his best cow yesterday?

He hasn't come up the yard since.

And I'll tell you another thing

leaning in to me,
folding down her apron
from the cotton noose
she lassoed from
her thinning neck,

she wrings
her hands tight,
keeps them to herself

and poor Victoria Beckham,

poor poor Victoria,

did you even get the news?

Jack

You're six foot tall
with shoes that need
their own hanger
and hands that go on
forever. Our best days
are spent watching
Comedy Gold and
putting fried food
on the table to eat.
I try not to mention
grades, sex, the body
or how many times
a day you boil the kettle.
I make an effort
to follow the football
closely on local news
and wait for the
transfer markets
to open for one-
sided chats. Hushed
monologues with
Ray go on forever
over talent and price
and my mood. This
year I will buy fifteen
blue and white
candy striped candles,
there will be no glitter,
I'll wonder who
deleted the years,
why they
passed so fast, scream
at you to tidy your room,
then squeeze
your narrow waist,
laugh at the cliché
we've both grown into,
thinking
you'd be any club's
greatest investment.

Egg

When the fourth doctor said

your son is an egg cracked by a hammer

I thought how no-one makes an
omelette
    without cracking

you heard the vicious
onomatopoeic word
as a terrible screaming

so now darlings

let us break everything up

(like she did to a life's work)

I offer you this

crack is needed to be born

ed is somewhat unfixable

therefore let us settle on the
hammer's potential
to build

Venturia Inaequalis

for Finn

The ingredients for success are not for sale on the shelf at Tesco or discharged
    into gold-foil bottles labelled *Drink Me*. More's the pity. The ditches are
overgrown with foxtail, cankery scabs feast our apple trees. You can never catch

a neighbour's eye on this road, but they burn *you should know better* tawdry tattoos
    on your back, and we trust we should keep Finn in on the driveway.
At eight it's a bit late to learn the ways pedals rotate out on the roadway.

Keep your eye to the horizon, don't look down, drop your leg to keep
    balance. As his coded Lego block drawers, we have maps of instruction branded
to his brain, 'safe-point' 'freeze-and-wait point' 'only-ask-a-woman-

with-a-buggy-for-help-point.' I pull then push his Minecraft hoodie-crease, trace
    my palm down his spine, a fuzzy overgrown fungus choking the tree-bark,
a naked struggle in his first incubator. *Is it harder to pedal when you have*

a disease? He screams. *You do not have a disease!* Narrow carcassy knees
    scattershot the handlebars. *I do, it's awesomeness or autumnness?* We know it's
autumn and our awe is full as the blooming apple tree promise. And to spite

the black angry spots, they will still fruit. They won't burst and beg to be
    plucked off their pregnant weight, we will scrub our harvest in a little
molasses and cider vinegar, bring up the skin-shine and peel the tiny crab

apples, splash them in an amber whiskey, sprinkle the flesh chunks in
    muscovado sugar drops. Then leave to soak. We can sweeten it.
We won't dig our tree up out of the ground. And we will sing you of our produce.

Journey West

1.

The road at Lorrha dips
to persuade us west
to hay makers and
silage wrappers.

The Shannon river
bursts bank for
Atlantic's magnetism.

We turn at the Ferry Inn,
a tin roof giving
rain drizzle
a landing place.

The grey slate stone,
predictable,
all shades darkened
on today of wet-wind,
as good lands mutate
to hungering scrag.

We cross the bridge
where an old man once
shoved a blue row
boat to her currents,
our skin summer-scuffed.

All the plebs
and St. Brendan
off on a
convert-to-happiness spin.

But my father's hapless
tuppenny sea knowledge
of currents and half winds,

had us rowing up and down river,
half-delighted
half-terrified
blown off course by
motorboats and modernity swell.

2.

The Portumna church
holds gaze on the corner.

And we're belting
home west
as a young Dunlin
searches out her nest.
Loughrea roundabouts
are a quagmire of
circular amadáns,
confusing the coots
and lugworms.

As Red Coat hunters
race trucks
on the new motorway,
swinging off at Kilconieron,
unsure of who they
ever were.

And us, creeping in the
ditch-water towards town,
turn in at Cemetery Cross.

My grandmother's
warm body in the cold ground.

And despite going west,
I will not plant flags
or find gold.

This work here is done.

Limestone walls built
vertical by men I never met
for time's inhospitality
and centuries' spontaneity
divides and conquers
for safety or shelter.

I have their triangular shape
wide shoulders, wide chest,
narrowing at the waist,

that's how we are recognised;
by shape and fist.

3.

The mart is in full throttle,
I choose not to hear
men speak from mouth corners
like dried up oysters,
lips sucked tight round secrets.

The auctioneer in a spin,
the way they like him.

And my father;
a man among men selling sheep
with coded bleats.

Hawthorn sticks to spines
crack through wool tufts,
they are worthless today,
as everyday.

4.

The offer of low fields is
a distraction and hiding place.
A wild and beautiful murmuration
of starlings and rooks opens theatre
to the descending caricature.

Miles of side-mouth-chat
happens along ditches with
rowan and blackberry bushes,
whispering ivy speaks to
the full lavender trees
and acres and acres
of conquering leylandiis.

The sales are in guineas,
apple trees, red trees and oaks,
car engines and animal feed,
creamery tins and grease
are currency and escape.

New streetlights confuse
young badger cubs,
shopfronts' sharp fonts
and frigid entrances
mean
I do not enter.

I am gauche and foolish —
as ever,
a lamb at pasture.

A seven-year stutterer.

My father in M. Glynn's Bar
near the North Gate,
where the markets' plenty
came in and out,

and people were graded
and degraded in ways we
reinvent at our borders
and barstools.

King John's Castle hall is cold.
The tunnel to the Friary is a rat's hovel.

5.

If I take you to the forge
on young ponies I rode out
the Tuam Road and
into the darkness,
the heartbeat rasp
mimicking
the rising trot,
the wire of their manes
cutting my soft knuckles,
the unevenness when
they'd break to canter
as school buses tipped
down to Lackagh,

I will be accused of poor plagiarism.

But I am certain of my truth.
And my half-truth.

How I see only
fear in the face of open flame,
the scalding embers
the hissing
and how man's jaw line
is so tight and vigilant.
Only sometimes my nervous
reflection is fretful,
the flame always
willing for combustion.

How a farrier lifts the
hoof by pulling
hard the hock hair.
All animals are volatile
yet docile.

The road home was
slippy in new shoes,
both of us unsure,
trotting past the
post office. Again.

And I note,
even in my sleep,
how hard young horses
blow out in excitement

as Friesians graze
on their knees in the snow,
trucks play Russian roulette
until the road sparks,
even in winter's sludge.

The mist in from Dublin,
a spurious flashback.

Easterly winds
are the strongest,
to keep us blown inwards
to show us our coordinates.

So that we never stray,
stay here, rooted
like hungering horses
fallen in at their flanks.

The fear of starvation is
always a constant
so easily resurrected,
to hell or to hunger.

So we stay muted and safe.

My small fist on
the rubber reins,
the horse's eye-white
making
its way to me in a
wild head thrust,
muscle tight,
a warning sign,
nostrils provoking.

Both of us afraid
of every shadow
especially our own,

until
we can see and feel
by only imagination.

Passing the rusted
yellow water pump,
I can only hear gurgle,

I am doltish,

breathe the smoke from
the small chimneys,
noise of our rebounding
in the empty,

and the road Home
welcoming and cold.

Definition

increase   begin again   get up   stand straight erect (erection)   incline   mountain   gain or get   lift   knock-a-laugh-or-a-**rise**   involve yourself in   revolt or a   revolution embryonic stage   shot/knock a bolt from the blue **rise** to rising   I am **rise**n   you are **rise**n he/she is **rise**n   awaken   succeed (at all costs   succeed seed growth)   to be duped (rarely/if ever/keep your fucken back to wall girl)   lift oneself (off your arse/settle bed/scratcher)   **rise** above one's self show disrespect   ascent (like Jesus)   an improvement   wheels coming off track   (perhaps in ice   drive into the skids)   more pay/wage increase/more beans/the big **rise** (aka the big job) one's cock   blood pressure   **rise** above one's station (the lord bless us)   knock a start out of something (even just your car engine) startle   to give yourself a good kick-in-the-hole   open your eyes   to come up for a breath   start with rising the eyelids   out of water/ pit/ hovel/ underground bunker/bushes   to loosely arouse yourself   move into   flow (like a river **rise**s on a mountain   or to menstruate) begin again begin again (fail) begin again (failed)   to keep going   to lift yourself out of the armchair   float to not be fucken dead a**rise**n   your future generation rising   **rise**ability factor   to bring the best of yourself to an occasion (or a challenge   e.g. make your granny happy)   sometimes borders on superior to improvise   hot air   outdo   just do feet on ground   feet off ground   to float keep your body in the air   hot air **rise**s   to not stay rooted   can return to life   be prominent (also used in dental chats)   increase   opportunity in your face   the emergence of a fish at the water's edge usually looking for food   (not as food)

two

'Go for the throat'
NICK LAIRD

The Harvest

There is nothing in the old Tuam beet factory only a greasy
fluthering of Natterer's bats and some gnawing weasels.

Once the full silos were emptied out, gathering began again
to bring in the next harvest, pregnant on a town promise of
those who plucked her beets from well-drained ground.

Bring your harvest to the side-door, ring the bell, check them in.

Throw away the bruised, pay the grower for the clean ones,
    pay the grower
for the fresh ones, for the ripe ones, give extra for pretty ones,
    weigh them.

Tip to piles making little beet hillocks, line them straight,
    singular,
inspecting with an old blackthorn stick, poke them, extract
    precious stone,
and sift the gravel, not for consumption. Burn the bitter,
    slash beets to cossettes.

Extract the inedible.

Cast them away over the ditch or take them to the pit in the
    dark of night,
move across the concrete slab, open it, side-step the weasels,
mind your ankle flesh. They'll eat the rabbits and the sugar and
god knows what, sitting on the slab spread-eagled and salivate.

It's rumoured they'll hunt you down out the Weir Road after your
matins, and midnight masses, naked of your cassocks, and rip the
cornea from your eyes, then feast on you.

They'll even come after your soul. And chew it. Refuse to release it.
Don't interrupt their funerals, they'll pull the skin from your
    hide and salt

all belonging to you, kneecappings and featherings as they
    cast a weasel spell.

Close over the concrete slab, quickly, blank your thoughts,
    bless yourself.

Don't look at the small skulls
Don't check if the hair is still growing
Don't take a deep breath. Do not breathe.

History Lesson

The Stone Age began around 10,000 years before Jesus came
    and made the Christians.
There were others too. Gods. Ages. Stones.

In 2010, a man tells me I shouldn't wear purple tights if
    I want to be middle management.

It's all about impressions and right now you're giving off a purple
    kind of flowery one.
Same with tattoos and piercings. Rotten teeth.

I keep the purple tights on my curved legs. I have no rotten teeth.
He keeps power. Mostly in his pants. He has a mouth of silver fillings.

My mother was born in a three-bedroom terrace in 1955.
She wanted to be the cowboy with a cap gun on the street,
Christmas Day.
She wasn't mad about the *injians*.
She never knew her history and it drives her mad.
She's a furious reader.
Taught me to be a furious reader. Read us endless stories.
Even stories that matched our birth dates.
They were my favourite. Her voice growing tired.

People began to farm and lay down roots and make cheese and
they say the first farm men were very clever men,
knew how to balance staying beside the sea and not getting wet.

My Nana brings digestive biscuits into the
London air raid shelter night after night.
Somewhere near St. Thomas's she said.
She calls her first son Thomas. My Dad.
He teaches me three things;

always drive into skid marks on an icy road.
He is the most important person in the world.

And when I'm not a cunt, I'm not too bad at all.
Honestly. All things considered.

Nana is glad of the break from slopping out shit buckets
    in the hospital.
She's not a hundred per cent sure who's dropping bombs
    on her,
but she likes the evening company. They sing songs.
    She loves to sing.

Her mother died when she was four from a burst appendix.
She's never been very sure of anything since except how
    she loves to sing.
And how very very tall and very handsome her father was.
She liked to drink brandy and smoke the odd cigarette.

I spent one full hour convincing some friends that women
    said poems in Ireland before
Eavan Boland. The women friends are suspicious.
    They have English degrees.

It's difficult to remember who first sailed around the
    Cape of Good Hope,
or of Storms, Diaz or Da Gama? But man's stealing stuff
    takes a Frankensteinian turn.
Or at least now some ass is keeping a logbook of all the
    bastarding things they can do to others.

This would appear to be a good thing.
Silk and spice being basic human needs,
like diamonds and bread and the internet and hoarding.

We can say for sure that Magellan proved the world was round even if;

a woman is laying under a sycamore tree
and watches a dappled grey horse gallop towards her,

steely long legs appear all of a shot, not making sense,
she is a long time pregnant, her nipples thick and dark.
Soon she will give birth, she knows the earth is round
as she sees the horse over her large belly.
It is all too sudden. It must be a ball.

And besides, Magellan died through his experiment.
But this is just a technicality.

She keeps this information to herself.
She doesn't believe in the many of their any gods.
And besides, she doesn't want to die for knowing stuff.

Christopher Columbus was a great man.

In the small salmon bedroom of her terrace house,
they put chloroform over my other Nana's nose on one
    of her eleven labours.
This child survives. She's thankful for not losing another child.
Do your duty. You must do your duty.
It is sometime in the 60s, she's not too sure. She was
    collapsed, she tells me.

Skip through Martin Luther, Jean Calvin, straight to the Jesuits.

We are all Roman Catholic. It says it on the school door.
We've cleaned up 'the abuses' with PR machines as
immovable as Croagh Patrick. We will ruin you in this town.
Protestantism allowed a randy king marry a younger woman,
stands for nothing but leaving your toaster out on the sink.

There was never really a Civil War in Ireland.
A few brothers had a fight, down in Cork or West Cork,
or actually I think it was Mayo.
Give it five minutes class coverage at most.
Actually I don't think you need to teach it at all, there's confession
    that day.

Michelangelo, Petrarch, Raphael, Dürer, now they were all great men.
I could go on. And on. And on. And I will.

2015 is the first year I read a comprehensive list of female
    Renaissance artists, Sofonisba Anguissola was a friend
    of Michelangelo. Bet he copied her.

*The Industrial Revolution was a great time, lots of great inventions,
made great by the Agricultural Revolution, lots of food to make
    the men great.*

Many women worked in the factories,
I don't know their names.
They only teach about a Spinning Jenny.
And I think this is named after an ass.

In 2007 a doctor tells me I have a brain clot,
I am pregnant, I ask him of the option of a termination.
He tells me that I will change my mind when I am a mother.
'I am a mother,' I say.

I heard three women's names mentioned in my History Class.
Nano Nagle, Constance Markievicz and Mary Robinson.
I try to imagine what they would do.

My first boyfriend punches me seven times on Shop Street
    and we end up in the hospital because he puts his fist
    through the window of a shop my uncle works in
    (bad coincidence). But I am in terror in case anyone
    has recognised me. The shame.

In 1927 women are banned from sitting on juries in Ireland.

History lessons. *In 1935 contraception is banned in Ireland.*

The hospital give me a card for domestic violence abuse victims.

I am embarrassed at how little they know about me.
And how much I can raise a man's temper.
And my poor ability to mind my men.
I put the card in the bin and withstand another year
for love.

I cannot mind my men. I keep this secret. For now.
I think of Mary Robinson again. I feel a bit of a shit.

It will take a decade before I realise I do not rise temper
    in anyone.
They rise all by themselves. This should be the first lesson.

Mussolini's rise to power was made easy by the colour of their shirts,
    the communists,
the Treaty of Versailles and his March on Rome.

I meet Ariana Reines for the first time in 2015. We drink
    ginger cocktails in a bar in Copenhagen, I promise I will
    use the word cock more in my work.
(cockcockcockcockcock)
    I still cannot come up with a proper name for my own
    cock area. I like the word cunt, but I like to use it angrily
    at those I hate.
(cuntcuntcuntcuntcunt)
    I am blown away by Ms. Reines,
    and how the paper won't refuse her ink. I only wish I met
    her sooner.

The 1916 Rising was neither a rebellion nor a revolution;
    it was a thing apart entirely.
It was a glorious thing, with god and glory and rising.

And look at us all now.

I ask my class why 1916 makes them happy?
They tell me it's better than being fucking English.
Although a few of them are English, but they like being Irish too.

The men often signed the Solemn League and Covenant in blood.

I correct the use of the word fucking as a race adjective.

I have never taught with an openly gay teacher.

Medieval times meted out some cruel punishments, most of which
   are still being perfected and used in the world today.
   Though most kids will come away thinking knights are cool
   and castles had great shooting windows and the past is the
   past and The Enlightenment, oh how enlightened it made us all.
   Particularly the men, who in turn could chose what to do with
   enlightening the women, and all the other races they had to
   deal with too.

Savita Halappanavar dies in October 2012. I cannot stop crying.

2017, My London Bombing Nana is dead and the
Salmon Bedroom Nana is trying hard to remember.

Oak

I'd like to spend Easter 2016
birdwatching on the Isle of Wight.
I will not be remembering shootings or blood. I will kill no bird.
I will not hunt and I will not cry. On Monday, I will set base camp
and patch my tent from the Plough and Stars.

A kindly man will tell me that westerly winds are prevailing and
I should pitch under a large shadowy oak tree and stretch out a
candy-striped windbreaker across my extraction point.

I will heed his warnings.

I will indulge my *Mick and me Fantasy* behind the furze bush,
I will wet my lemony green tea behind the shadowy oak tree.

I'd have no trouble shooting people dressed up in my ghillie suit.
Saving someone is far harder than shooting them dead. Save or shoot?
Roll up! Roll up! Meet ya half way? Any chance of a luck penny? Isn't war a whore?
All the best with the power sharing though powerful people don't like to share.
Good luck with the hurt-remembering, dead-finding, peace scavenging.

I will slowly sip the tea as a penalty,
a punishment, my own gentle firing squad. I don't like lemons much.
There'll be no jaw jacking, just supping.

When night falls on the plough and illuminates the stars, I will low crawl from
my tent. I will tell of Echo to the Nightjar, share nibbles of shame with some
Woodcocks, the Long-Eared Owl might hoot at me to *Give over about Victor,*
and by nightfall I'll delight in the Less-Spotted Woodpecker, knowing she
can damage just tapping ever so gently gently gently *alpha bravo charlie*

      until
      the
      tree
      dies
      and
      we
      relax
      deep
      into
      the
      dark
      bark
      hole

on the nature of things

1

these streets sing songs of the last voice
oh rebel your dead skeleton ballads still echo
the River Liffey is a Yeats painting

sepia frantic flailing

red wine is now slurped from black wooden troughs

we've drunk a revolution into dry stains
along streets   neighbours bleat
still keep feet in everyone's business

the revolution lost is whitewash bleach
a mother's missing son a foetal figure
with other bridge dwellers

the revolution won perched at
chipboard desks
explaining how it is

                      good | bad
            and so it is and must be
       for gods of their concoction

2

                  rising gun shots
                  the bulge of the eyeball
                  he ties boot laces
                  stunned by bullets
                  he's wearing short pants

a tall woman with pram says
himself is in some
battle with the Germans down in trenches
she flinches   repeats it

sick from the baby's mouth is wiped fast;
a smoky rag
kids' hot blood is at her feet

3

the cobbles make noise now only from memory

a century knuckled by
silenced the women and

blood can always paint your
windowpane-boxes speckled ruby-red

never forget
so patriots, what will hydrate

our wedding bed sheets now
we have no beds to lie in?

as devastation crumbles breeze blocks
the creaking ghost estates haunt our sleep

surely we could give shelter to the rebels and their children?

4.

our revolution is now a mother missing from her
hoodied boy as he blitzes pages from
Blood on the Rose

she tells her sister how he's out of control
but she hopes he's not cold

half formed sounds spitting out the words

using finger pads under the bullet text
graphite stains he licks could make supper

his wanton dimples are our disgrace

at the back gate of Trinity
I cross the road to go again
to *The Taking of Christ*
to see myself in Judas
with red lippy, *heroine shade*

a ripped centaur blindfold on my eyes

kid's green sleeping bag
lairing anaconda coils
round young ankles
sprouting virgin hair

his quiet words are wet kissed vowels
passing through an open mouth
to the dogged Dublin delay

                and our wet new tongues
                cannot say to speak
                what they want to say
                nor what they should say

Alternative Truth

post **truth truth** after dinner pre **truth** alternative **truth truth** without fact respect the **truth** there'll be **truth** in my house **truth** victim **truth** orphan do you know the **truth** tell the **truth** canon law **truth** my **truth** is there any **truth** to be had chicken soup for the soul **truth** the winner's **truth** the undeniable **truth** the **truth** of my life the second **truth** the biblical **truth** check your sources **truth** cursed relic **truth** medical diagnosis **truth truth** before bed **truth** in the morning child's **truth** delusional **truth** upsetting the fuck out of everyone **truth** car crash two tales both true **truth** I swear to tell the **truth** the whole **truth** and nothing but the **truth** the skirt was short **truth** consent **truth** we'll be serving **truth** any minute now in the parlour the kind **truth** delivering **truth** the **truth** of the rabbi the sun worship **truth** the naked **truth** the dealer's **truth** gut wrenching **truth** the coma **truth** the **truth** in your dreams colonial **truth** the **truth** of my tale delete the **truth** mute **truth** define **truth** write the **truth** down braille **truth** moral **truth** stone raving mad **truth** water **truth** organic **truth** one hundred per cent sustainable **truth** global warming **truth** punched in the face **truth** white collar **truth** any tribunal's **truth** tracker mortgage **truth** I have your best interests at heart **truth** there is no heart beat **truth** there is brain activity **truth** life saving **truth** the water is deep **truth** lock the doors **truth** college campus **truth** upsetting the fuck out of everyone with no filter **truth** sworn to secrecy **truth** friendly fire **truth** the **truth** of language **truth** spy **truth** sly **truth** deniable **truth**

after Sarah Clancy

The Apology

Flags and blood banners
hang from tarred motorway poles,
a sectarian hangover.
A heavy thick fog
chokes up the Belfast backstreets.
The traffic lights confuse me,
yet the motel is as every
bleak mid-American traffic stop.
Late after the reading a row
erupts like stink violet gas
from the Trifid Nebula;
Heaney fucked over the Beats
he lived a war,
and we got bog craft mystery.
I threw those handy stones,
I stuck my long nailed hand
to your bleeding side and
I purred
kissing your cheek.
I should have known better.
My mother taught
better manners
than to hurl myself along
fast highways with bandit fools.

The Management of Savage Chaos

Dear World of Chaotic People,

Hit soft targets, creep round in the dark, shame works well, keep it there, just under your skin, despair the prisoners into madness, you may have to feed them to negotiate a swop, do it cheaply, best thing you can ultimately do is never look in their eyes, or down at their hands, even while tying them, this will put you off torturing them, you might see your mother's shadow, this can throw you off centre, and is a double negative, it negates itself, so you might in fact be just grand, love and hate, life and death, fire and water, fuck and fuck-off. I'm not going to go fully into double negatives now, kill and die, die and dead, live and life, as they won't be successful for chaotic imaginings, they could make you doubt yourself, and what would we do, let us not startle chaos of a savage nature, whatever you do, bless yourself or fall to your knees, best if the media see the women crying, it's better if we see the children dying, although this can also work against us, so take care.

Dear World of Decent People,

You have wet grass under your feet, you can only sow food there, this in itself is not a sure thing, but it can be. If you are standing on sand, build up. All you have are the arms that wrap around you, you can use your own. You may have a front door of a house or the flap of a tent or hedgerow hole. And if that bangs in, all you have are the thoughts in your head. They are in you, wherever you hold them, (in your guts your head your heart). The enemy can scorch everything else, but they can never burn what you know. Even if they cremate you. Bury you. Dump you out to sea. They can never touch what you feel. Or who felt you. This will frustrate them, chaos never succeeds. Though it tries hard. Theory favours it. But this beautiful secret. It will never succeed. This is only for you, only you need to know this.

Moderato

After Sergei Rachmaninoff

On
    the
        Volkov
            River
              I
                push
                    my
                      oar
                        to
                          the water

          I am learning to row myself to air.

Yelena, I too am pale and thin now and I am not made for
    the sureness of our people and the fickle blood that runs
    through us both.
Grandmother is well, fussing in that idle way she does and
    forever feeding me.

Heavens! She screams, *you must not be like your sisters,*

                                      eat

                      eat

          eat

    eat

I know food won't bring back little Sophia. I tell her this in
    the dark, and I can
never see Father returning again to us with knish and dressed
    herrings,
his head back, laughing, *Sergei you must eat before playing boy!*

Yelena, I know you are dead, I only pretend when I'm
    rowing to have you there
and Sophia too, but I know death. So I must write my
    breaths
into these keys. I promise I will not eat until I have served you.

Getting the Priest for Roethke

for Kieran Day

Once I climbed through
walls to wake the priest
for Roethke

I was five

Roethke had the fear

priest came out dressed
like a swan in heat
rushing out the Bofin shore

to him

who had the horrors

the fear

I could see the
paisley pyjamas collar
winking from the chasubles

their four eyes
balling at each other

priests only
like to be
woken for
the dues or
the dead

I said, quietly
to the ground

not woken violently
for the sweat lathered Roethke
or the poems
mad in his head.

Sinéad

If we question where love is hidden,
we must imagine where hate goes
when it freezes. I imagine it is locked
in an abandoned railway station.

You have all the tarnished warriors
on the quick tip of your tongue
and you have charred yourself in
the flames of a hellish Hades
and faced down Persephone
on a daily basis

and recovered from the brink
of their madness enough times
to know there aren't different
parts to anything.

That even science can be wrong.
That a star isn't shattered for
our sensitivities.

What should be and could be
has no translation in the
Irish you speak.

Right is right and
wrong is a trap door's loose hinge
to burn your enemy alive
with the sharpest of minds.

If you ever set an army out the
Dublin Road to recover our past,
marching beside the old St. Pat's gate
up as far as Costcutter,
carrying curried chips
in those calf boots you
wear on cold days,
I'll join you.

For you could topple
the world right side up
like Sojourner said,
and you would demand it.

We wouldn't debate it.

It's well and good to
pander polite pronunciations
in the comfort of a parlour.

(A habit you're not entirely convinced of)

When it comes to war,
it's always urgent.

The clear road back
is a clear road out.

There is only one route.
There is only one journey.
There is never time to debate in a hurry.

You either think all humans matter.

Or you don't.

There are Blooming Daffodils in December

I pick one for my mother and
find her above in the top field
looking for berried holly.
She puts the run on me with
my fresh yellow offering
in winter's sun.
Run, run, we laugh.
It's the Winter Solstice.
It will turn to warm yellow soon
and we will run out of breath.

three

*'Does my sexiness upset you?
Does it come as a surprise
That I dance like I've got diamonds
At the meeting of my thighs?'*

MAYA ANGELOU

Muse

A man I would
like to fuck.

A woman I would
like to fuck over.

Amuse

A woman I would
like to fuck.

A man I would
like to fuck over.

I am not a Bog Queen or a Fig or a Pomegranate

1.

Friday opens with a caesarean cleave, the scalpel's held over me,
  so I hide
myself under a tattered eiderdown for the greater parts of the day
  and only

spread my ideas and hysteria to my mother, whose love is the kind
  I hurt.
And all the day long the mad barking of dogs in my neighbour's
  tin shed drives me wild.

I have lived here all my life, despite delicate jaunts to plant
roots elsewhere, new neighbours, down subways, smoky air,
  but my body gives up her act,

trips me, tongue loses tautness, so I stay, stare out the back window,
eyeing the coarse pig weed and quack grass colonising
  the lawn,

old shed doors are coming undone at rusty hinges,
  yet under the
white arches at the front of this home, I attend the trailing
  lobelia as it spews

from wicker hanging baskets. Our window dressings are
  staunched and
bandaged for the world. And so to you my lover, I have fantasised
  about your touch

since dawn, with its patience. We squandered our words
  last Sunday, after our
rampage of domesticity and I started my long retreat,
  my arsenal of rusty weapons

[you have immunised against] pussing, skulking, punching walls.
   Hybrid dinosaurs on the black screen break up the silence,

fried greasy duckling wings from last night's dinner stop
   spitting in the pan,
the postman catches a glimpse of my motley eiderdown
   shield, my parakeet eyes behind it,

and he knows my secrets, like how only green eyes change
   colour
in fear, so I loudly sing, *all I want is and all I need is to
   find somebody.*

I boil water for Pot Noodles, then offer the children vitamin
   tablets shaped like
gummy bears, compensation for the lack of food and
   mothering and all the crying.

Knock at the door. Let me touch your hand. Just once.
   I miss my father today and his
smell under this mad mantle and I miss too you and your
   smell. I miss men.

2.

There. I said it. It has been written down in bullet ink.
   I miss them and I lay siege
behind this shield, crying. There I cry too. This too is
   written down.

I will never ever write this Friday into a poem. Some will tell
   me it's not
poem'y 'nuff stuff. In their language. That language they made

and expect me to communicate in. In the language of puffed
   chest and sharp look to stare, crow's feet, of stubble and

solution and doctors. We might, though, sit by Sunday to make
up a new lover language. Ok. Begin. Again. Code. Love. Child.
    Fear. Sweat.
Forgive. SOS. Save me. I'm drowning so fist in the air, don't wave,

I will think you are saying *hello*. Come. Come. Come and be
    in me, near me, on me. Our language will be the language
of hand. Of your touch to my face.

In this cave we dwell in over a mad ocean of undercurrents,
    take shelter under
the flaky lip of this eiderdown cliff, practice pronunciation of
    patient deliberation and

cup-washing. I promise you I will have no talk for father.
    And the great purple
Calluna heathers will bloom. I might be mithered at times.

I see that angst on strangers' faces down streets too. I hear it
    on our lanes,
outside disco clubs at three am, screaming soft sad madness
    to each other,

you fucked him with your eyes. I will dream of nine current man muses,
    listening to Dylan, the vinyl's edge pierced by the pin
you make loooove just like a woman but you cry like a little girl.

Repeat. I will correct his mistruths,
    kernels formed from cribs and days we cut our knees skin deep

and the days we walked ourselves into hardwood doors,
    days we went out late into night
wearing pumps to run from rape or towards lustful
    dew-drunk mornings,

as rowboats came in full of oysters and clams down off
    Quay Street or down by the
Rowing Club near the fastest moving river. I make love
    like a woman.

I don't need this sung at me, repeating. I make love like
    a woman. I cry like a woman too.
My girl is long swallowed in that fast river, the bowels
    of the Corrib,

swept out to sea. But you have cross-stitched your boy to
    your safe dermis. I know he's there.
But I will not sing you of it. Shaming you.
    I will write it out in secret.

I keep my many muses. My loves. And I am not absurd
    for my strong lusts.
All these fragments, driftwood, bog-oak, fire-pits,
    chipped-bone, are all bits of me.

Temper. Strong jaw-line. Fear.

There. It too is written down.

In Montmartre with Degas

Who owns these hips   these awful saucer over-lacquered eyes
and abandoned pink-jellyfish-on-the-rock lips   this harsh-one-layer-mono
does nothing for my double chin   but you already know that

I'm no ballet dancer   my delusions a smelting loss|love   me ever on parole
but that mendacious muff and wiggle-butt is *way* off   stuff it
down your tight pants   I note though   how a citrine sun makes me smile

       and I softly come at midnight   once in a while on Beaujolais
and someone's hard hands to roll up my   dried tiny tobacco leaves
leaves a yellow-after to stain to my teeth   your fingers crunch-roll it

       like when I was much younger and could pivot like a dancer
but you never believe that story   though I've told you a thousand times
like this stinking oily fish on the zaffre and white enamel dish is rotting in the sun

       behind the Louvre doors I lie nude on the furs and wax coats
stinking of musk and man and dead and fowl and what
is past and to come is only the rapid   shortening of breaths

and more certain of my last escape as I am left on your canvas   wobblyfull
and whole   I keep thinking I should walk out   or walk back

In the Garage with Degas

The breeze blocks and perspex roof   bring out goose pimples
the kettle measures volume in a torrid yellow oil slick on the bloated side
that's how they take tea out here   the mechanic's lamp dangles off a

powdered orange nail   so Bauhaus brittle
a large chain hoist for pulling engines from cars is cloaked overhead
a calf jack in the oily corner   almost apologetic

the lamp's bulb is skin like trapped in an unloved electric earthworm   hasn't
brought light since I was five   and dropped it in a
weak manoeuvre beside a   Cortina with a gammy clutch

while a man shouted out names of things I didn't understand or could ever reach
now in the dark   Degas tells me to prepare myself   be brave   we can re-own
everything   especially body   car   cow   politic

we're going painting   and though he's upset at my
Picasso tattoo   he promises not to misrepresent me
this is a new space   we've up cycled

even the page three women are turning septic sepia behind the press for style
to fit in   as he turns their image away from us
juggling breeze-block brushes made to paint fences not faces   so he

promises not to blame his tools for making a rounded belly   languorous hips
double chin   and he giggles as the overalls are catching him
I try on a welding mask   hiding blind   not a spark

         and he doesn't notice the shaking of my mulberry-mottled wrists
    the skin on this ballet dancer's foot breaking through my swelling hoof
the curve of my waist   nothing of how real women remember

not noting how memory is etched in the corners of their lips
                            or how night's mossy breath
    made me disappear   out of sight

Pushing the Body

Pushing her fleshy hips
through imaginary space
with a thick Northern accent

doesn't make people afraid.
It makes them stand back
as drift wood on a silver beach,

a kite let loose from
the hand of a small boy,
blood rubber steering wheel

alone in the long grass
after jack-knifed wheels
have danced to the ditch.

She's the decorated
Indian elephant
at an arranged wedding feast.

Your Belly is Full of Girl

child and your kitchen bins
haven't been emptied since Friday

           when tectonic plates
                      crashed near Nepal

limbs fell asunder like lamb shank strings on your mother's heavy crockery

                      Daddy
                      broke us

  in in in in in in in in in in

                      to
                        little
                        pieces

waxy doll
        her young limbs
   arm   from

                                        arm

   [and who will mind her from harm now?]

        who
        will
        put a
        steel
        crow
        bar to
        the
        shaking
        plates

   before they smash and blow and
   break the house and we find her
   under the heavy kitchen table?

and i hope that i don't fall in love with you

you could have gone to ground
or spent   yourself   to seed
like a dying   coriander plant

deeds of decency rulebook:
        one   hibernate the winter outlaw

        (i might forget you in the dead lapse)

        two   store up your stockpile

        (eat the sweet september berries first)

        three   fall asleep and cause no fuss

        four   see rules one through three
                      (forget me)

i know what's good for us

but then you show up in ikea out of the bluest blues
    (without permission)
lying
      on a single bed

next you're drinking whiskey-and-sancerre-iced-sours-with-a-fucking-gorgeous-adam's-apple-bobbing-at-me-in-the-bierhaus

      i snapped on my turquoise speedo goggles but I could
        taste you in the
                                  lingering
                                  lime peel
          stuck between my front teeth

    i wrapped a blindfold over my eyes but i
    stopped the blood flow and fell over

      i stole my mother's yellow sleep-mask to stop the
      light banging through my retinas and creating
    upsidedownimages

then there you are on the street of all random places and i really
thought you should have ducked into mcdonald's and shirked my
frankenstein walk up augustinian street   bought yourself a

fillet-o-fish   my eyes

                swathed

my hands madly clamping onto your chest

and i hope that i don't fall in love with you
i hope that i don't fall in love
i hope that i don't fall
flat on my face

later i promise i will drip hot red wax on my eyelids
    to seal them
        or perhaps superglue, you need to do the same
            and we probably need to shove it up our nostrils too

if you had only shimmied behind the bar leaned down low
restocking the merlot and pint glasses   before the damage

the lipstick stains   *mac garnet berry* in case you need it on reorder
but it was festival chic limited supply that i inked on your jaw so
    it's out-of-stock
you could have done the decent thing and pretended you lost
    some sterling coins on the sawdust floor   swatted me away
                    kept your eyes to yourself

    or gouged them out with the lemon pick and packed the holes
        with a salt poultice
                                            kept me safe
you will squire page
but never knight
                    bloom to seed
                    bad deed in never heeding me

and i hope that you   *in love with me*
                    fall

The **BANKSY** Girl

I am talking about you in Spain
I am talking about you in a church

I am talking about you in Porto di Trieste

watching   SHIPS FLOAT   in

I bawl whisper about you in the Jacks
I am giving **out**   I **scream** out under the gap in the door looking for loo roll
I am giving out about you under the steel spire on O'Connell Street
I curse whisper your name to a shiny Copenhagen swan + tell her
pedal fast girl, get home soon, don't let the moon go down. Again

I am letting you down like the kid who ducks to the lake to retrieve an orange wool glove mother pulls her back by the blonde ponytail that matches father + brother + mother = the glove is coarse and wet-wool-nasty

I am letting you   in towns with no love
Down

up
I am letting me   I am **FLOATING**

I bite my tongue until it bleeds I try to chew it off but I am a **coward**

I cannot deflate myself by biting my tongue
I tried to wash my tongue with carbolic soap but it made so many bubbles and they came down my nose. I was hoping I would drown. I know this was foolish because I am a fool
You **TOLD** me

I am **screaming** out loud and a man grabs my mouth+shoves my
head into a bath

You are a cunt he says

but I know this, I have been warned before

they told me when I was kicked into **FAST-DREAMING** on the
pavement opposite the post office with my shoulder out of its socket
and they were kicking a good man up the street, they had counted
out our feat like you'd goose-step a death plot, I like post offices
I remember thinking, my teeth loose in my head
because I like getting letters

but I heard it   **cunt**   an air invasion of gritty stone
= familiar

when I was **8** I thought it was a pet word
when I called all my dolls **cunts**
when I called myself a doll just to fit it on me like an awkward childish dress
but I wasn't a *doll*

no one told me of Sojourner Truth or of Maud Gonne
or made dolls of them, they laboured dead men's names at me
and told me the women would ready things for me

orange segments, lemon pies, **ships in green glass bottles**
school-bags, *cerise pink lustrous hair ribbons*
pork chops and potatoes

they screamed them at me, so I hung them men on the walls in
FRAMES, and to the dolls, well I undressed them and I ripped their arms
free of their plastic sockets and left armholes and pulled off their legs
and said **you look better this way** with your legs and arms
astray in the cot

a strange beautiful man calls me darling in the mildew night
and I can see cloud reflections in the puddles at my feet, I know to
never look up, never look up, keep your feet on the ground, he
throws me **off-centre**

it's been an eternity of nights since I've been thrown
off-centre and I hate it

darling I say back to myself
you fool, if only you knew

you should call me   **cunt**   not
darling

he told me   **you** told me   they told me

I know all the things you told me, and I learned them off
by my heart
It saves my life sometimes

and when I walk away I do not sleep the night again
and all I remember is the night you said you loved me
that I was a good girl
that I had made you proud and I kissed your old skin
I **floated** home

it was summer
I was the **BANKSY** girl

but **BANKSY** is only a fake tattoo   nothing to me

and I less to you

Player

And now that I am Geras,
I see nothing in the Beautiful Game,
but potential in their chest cages
and how they might arch their backs
for me in the dark.

The Marriage

After he half-arsedly lassoed her with a yellow gold ring, confetti promises, guests ate grapefruit rings with mini cherry toppers, a morning suit sizes too small for even the wiriest frame. A Josh-Ritter-look-a-like after Golden Age of Radio, she was Pretty Princess Sad-Frost, no fun, and she was starving from eating only raw eggs to fit her hips to lace. Thatcher on a campaign trail to victory as she was falling down the stairs more times than he cared to remember. But now they were married and bed-wed.

The first time I caught a wedding bouquet, it fell flat on my Doc Martens. I kept my hands in my pockets, kicked up an orange lily powder dust that dyed onto the boot soles that could withstand oil, fire and heavy-duty petrol bombs, but not the piercing corsage needle that stuck to my chest years later. Not the great mad abyss of leaping into *forever*.

Inventor

I made myself new.

    I gave myself Marilyn eyes
    and a light tongue.

I melted on a laminated hand,
so unlike
    the one I dug turf with

    used to carve my name
    to tree bark

    that fixed the electric
    wing mirror back onto the Mazda
    after a morning's driving rage.

Guilt and the past made my hands
so useful.
But unattractive.

Bog-like and pathetic,
    he said,
or just really funny.

I was The Queen of Hearts,
I didn't forge myself fingers.
You don't need them
as a suit of shiny perfect

I stopped driving the roads raging,
I carved new hips, a waist, and a pretty smile
and I gave away my smarts and good intentions.

And while I'd smile at bar stool men,
    I'd stop sitting there,

never let my roots grow out too black

but this was a short lived invention
only idiots live like this
so I started over

and I made new and I made new and I made new.

Dystopia

night so dark   the clouds were
coming down on us
and she said
we can cut them back with scissors
and a day so black   the night was
always present
and she said
we can slice it with this   knife
alive   I have one
in my apron pocket
and all the while of tumbling
      we sliced
day to night to day to night
and the child in her belly
would too be safely sliced
to air
                to a thick fog
of the world   a suet of activity
a sludge   they think world
resembles womb but it doesn't

there is no such thing as womb
there is woman and organ
uterus   brain   lung   skin
heart   they can
do good   or
sometimes they can   kill her

till you all know this
we will carry sharpened
blades in our   apron pockets

four

"Is there no way out of the mind?"

SYLVIA PLATH

Wrongheaded

1 | Hand Fast |

The women are here to count
    To sit together and carve out arms
To bury their dead   to feed their living
    When they are done they
Dance in the end clutches of their spat energy
      Bone on bone   sharp cuckoo barrage

Sweet desire

All spent

2 | Liquescence |

How to Contour the Face to Make Things Pop

Use a primer. Wash on generously. Lather. Then begin by painting forehead bone, next the temples, sides of nose, chin, and hollows of cheeks with iridescent highlight. Next, with Lavinia Fontana's stroke as she puts the belly on Cupid and the nose on Venus, flick straight brown lines parallel to them. Buff, bust and burst the brush to sfumato the skin, we must all blend in. And without moving the tiny face hairs far, keep small tight circles, stay in a small circles, remain moving the wrist, but keep it tight, sweep, cover and accentuate the cheek bones, although this face is so thin now, perhaps best to consider plumping it out with a pop of colour: *Love Lorn*, *Girl about Town*, *Likeable* or *Milan Mode* are all delicious pinks for bringing back life to a dead pallor. No need to curl the eyelashes. The eyes will be closed.

3 | **Vanishing** |

And if they have any spirit left
                                      They know to save it for one
   Another   they will only feel by leaning back
                                  Upon each other

     Mapping done deeds   Paying heed to their needs

   Breathing
              Screaming
Thawing   Melting

4 | **Kaleidoscope** |

    Through the dead window
The grey goose dirty pavement
    Floats to the mottled sky

Moves to meet your love

I think of how fast you moved into me
And how suddenly out of me

    My hipbone is lower
Down than yours
    It sits in your knee groove
And sometimes I like us to walk this way
    Dragging you with me

Dragging me with us, our
    Three-legged walk down
The soused empty streets

And sometimes I don't

      Sometimes I can't. Today I can't imagine
Like now
Here, where you cannot find me

Where you cannot birth for me, or see my dreams.
The subtle cavities inside of me, I can hide things from you.
Like in a quiver. Or swallow my screams in the lovefucked
      Velvet folds
Here where I cannot find you, I can see you on the street
I see you walking away from me, or are you walking
      Towards me?
When we pause and freeze, I cannot determine this

And I tell you the tales, now, to remind you,
How oftentimes I am feeling all by myself

And especially now

To remind you why I scream when you catch another girl's eye
It's because of now

Now I am protoplasm
      Now I am organic matter
Now I am a weighty ion for you all

5 | Petrification or Condensation |

Spring is overused. I am overused. And you are
      Overawed
We are gnawed and wrapped and spat out and sucked in
      Magnetic
           Directions

      My nerves are at me
And I don't want a blue plastic tray
      I don't want to have to say to him
To you; all the hefty cleave of me

Go out; go out again to the outside
    Sneak your body out there
For me, if you slim yourself
    There are things I need
That you need to fetch for me, or him
    Maybe we just need to forage together
But you don't understand the word *forage* as I mime it
    Beside the edge of the bed, my hands going
Like the clappers, and the TV's gone to snow and shadows
    And I never can accept *together* in this ward
This is my space, and I don't want it. Despite having it

Space

The *I'm in his debt* space

6 | St. Vitus' Dance |

If you could go out to the outside and find me some air, I would be most grateful. I would hate to make a nuisance of myself but I would be so thankful. Although *I'm in debt to you for giving me air to live* would be the worst kind of debt. Myself should let me out. To the air. I should drive myself. To wherever. I cannot believe the care is such that I'm better in here where I cannot make a rule. I cannot find my keys. And I know I need them for escape. A decision. A cup-of-tea. My womb. This room is a cell. I am made of cells. My eyes. My finger tips. My shinbone. This womb makes madness of the rest of us. And the test of us is to just go get to the outside and breathe the air. And be without a care of everyone or anyone. This brouhaha womb. This woman womb. This honey fungus hole.

    You'll fit out through, I promise you
Here, take these tips:

First:

The narrow wooden knots in the door
    Push them through, push. Push
Push down and they will fall out
    Push hard down on the door's pine knots
And we'll be finished here, or there
    Either way, I am relieved when it ends

Second:

    You can bring the outside in
I miss the outside but you'll have
    To go grab it for me, quick
Kiss it hard and hold it inside your belly
    Quickening. A pennyweight
Of air. Whoosh. Quick. Quickening

Third:

Blow the green bright mossy outside into me. See. Simple

Me. Here. Here I am. Me. Here see. See me. Here. Here I am. Me

    Bring me the outside wind, and I can
Move, the wind will move inside of me
    I will find the middle,
It will force
    Into me, it calms my gimcrack nerves

Some times. Sometimes it calms me
Other times it frays me. Othertimes

Listen to me, ssshhh, get the outside and blow
    It back to me. Hurry

7 | Petrified | Hardening | Permanent |

Ssshhh, you shouldn't say that
Ssshhh, try get some sleep

If you leave your head back on the pillow
    And shut down your eyes

You're too erratic   You're nervous
You're too anxious
                 You're ectoplasm/desperate
You're too cautious

You're so suspicious chatty/weighted/loaded/charged

You're   so   giddy

You're too unclear

You're near   You're rushed

You're so slow   You're fucking needy

You're too demanding

You're so super
          You're quiet, why so quiet?
                     You're all hysteria

You should just ssshhh

And shut the creased frost violet lids
    Your young tired eyes — you might sleep
My love and ssshhh — maybe you can't say that
I shouldn't
    Have said it, I know
I know that now, but they didn't tell me
    They never told me

8 | Sucking Numb |

They didn't tell me to pack it in the bag
    I know they shouldn't have to constantly
Explain shit to me but
    I have all the pamphlets here
Look, nothing about it at all

D and C   if your child needs to be ventilated   what to pack for the labour ward   signs of meningitis   how fucked you are   how happy you are   how to get the paper cup from the coffee machine   where to order quinoa   where to have a ciggie   signs of dilation   tips for reducing piles   sit on an inflatable ring   clean hands save lives

See? Nothing about me. See? Or how to get the air back inside?
  Me

Ssshhh
        Or you and me

    But I'll stop now. I'll stop now

Sorry. I should stop now. Sorry. I am sorry you know. Sorry

Did the bottom of my back just snap?
    Would you mind awfully checking it for me?
I'm like a hawthorn stick, I am, see I'm brittle like this

    Ssshhh, maybe if we could say it
In another way, maybe it's the words
    They can't hear, is the air blowing
On your face yet, from the outside
    Did you catch it for me, to breathe it?
Through my body, you'll need more, you need to
    Suck it down into here, here, here, where it
Stretches out your hipbones darling
    Nonononono I can't feel it
Spray it on me, or move it to me
    Ssshhh, maybe if we're silent

9. | Kick Up a Dust |

I had never met him before
    I can't see your face mother, bring it
To me, bring it over to me

    I could put this crinkled cherry band
To your hair and it will pull the wisps of your strain
    Back into to the crown of you

> *I could tell you how he fucked me*
> *How I fucked him. How I liked it*
> *How he smiled. I think he liked it too*
> *But I won't tell you mother*
> *I have no better word than 'fucking'*
> *So I'll ssshhh. And how it was a cock*
> *And I am a hen in this den to crew*

I remember when you were born
    Here on the tiled rubber
Right here. Right by where you are now

Were you happy mother?

Yes. A little then. Not so now darling, and it's all
    Ahead of you my darling
Ssshhh. You have to stop. You have to stop screaming
    You have to stop asking
There is only one way to get
    Air in and get air out
No mother, there are more ways. There are always more ways

    They won't like you if you keep up your fuss

You're very pale like a bad duck egg darling
    Do you like duck eggs?

10 | **Enflame** |

There's a ring of sinewy stuff stuck in the middle of me
     Twisted tight, like rock, they're going
To take a hairy skin hammer to it and open the middle
     Of me. No they haven't asked me. It's not mine
I shouldn't have said that. They're only trying to help get
     To the middle of me and give me
Something, a ball of heather, a ball of heat, a ball of sunrise
     The ball moon, ping-pong of rain
The ball of middleme

11 | **Compliance** |

Ssshhh. I'm sorrysorrysorrysorrysorrysorrysorry. I would have drawn a map on vellum. I should have drawn a star. I could have put me on a bar graph or an app or something, and I would have let you find me, the middle of me, quicker, I see now how much I'm slowing down your day, holding up your trolleys and beds and catheters and toast for other mother makers. I could have jotted down coordinates and put them in some new soft wear. But I was doing the laundry and making bread. I'm sorry. I loved him, the very essence of his eye. I never found the middle of him, they never showed me how. It wasn't there; it wasn't fair that I never did it for him. I will hurry up. If I got up and walking, but I've a hose in my back. Ok if I stopped talking. I've said I'm sorry. I'm like the echo of the hills. I'm like the sorry of the cliffs. I mean the caves. My words are stumbled.

Have you found the middle of me? Of any of us?

This is the twilight hour
     Everyone dies at this hour
Nononononono he's fine, he's alive
     It's just devoid of energy, this hour.

Listen, he's clawing up through you, you know, or down
 Which way do you look at it?
Backwards

Like looking at the enamel casing of a looking glass

I had a looking glass once, in the shape of a teardrop

    I have never seen a fully formed teardrop
Do you not make them? In your eyes?
    Do your eyes not make them?

    No, I do, I make lots of them
I just never catch them fully formed
    They're like melting snowflakes

I fear I have cracked it when I got up too fast
    In a too fast motion, the looking glass
I did, I definitely did, and I cracked the casing
    And I chastised myself. For I was
Always breaking things, the wooden legs of our heron
    And that glass bottle that had the boat in
Smashed that too and your
    Yorkie easter egg mug

I would have packed it for you my love

The boat? No. The looking glass
    Even with the crack? Because of the crack

Am I cracked? Not yet darling. You've a few hours left

Were you happy looking into the looking glass?
    Well not with the crack in it
Was it cracked on the enamel part?
    Yes darling. But surely it wouldn't
Affect your reflection? Everything affects your reflection

12 | Honey Sac |

The light reflects the flats sprawl in the Liffey
The sun reflects my child's hair dyed blood colour red
The moon reflects our shiny oiled chimney breast
The stars reflect the ebony dashboard, with my feet elevated
The Christmas lights reflect chestnut eyes, only in my head

The looking glass will reflect your demise

But look, we have made it passed 12 labours with our feet up

13 | Ice Cubes for the Ferry Trip and Purgatory |

I wonder how many party bags of ice it would take?
    For what?
To keep her body frozen on the back seat of our car
    To keep her frozen in your beating stone heart
To not ever again reflect the stars
    Never
No never. To never again reflect the lights on the riverbed
My dead child
    Never? No no never
2. 2 what?
    2 bags
2 bags of what?
    2 bags of ice to keep it frozen

14 | Gentlemen's Agreement over Bouclé Coat |

I reached my leg over. Feeling the dark. The railings. Of the River Liffey. It was dark. Dead dark time. Deathly dark time. I put my second leg over. I was wearing a skirt. The frost sprayed pole shocked me. I am here. I am there. I am never inside my own head. I stepped inside the railing. Two men passed in Bouclé coats. They said are you ok Hun? No, I said. Can we call anyone for you? Yes, I said. Yes. Have you a number. No, I said. Have you? No, they said. Would you like our coat? Does it fit two? I said. His does, they said, mocking our new friend. It's very cold love. The railing. I know. I'm riding it. I'm frozen, I said. I am riding it straddle. Not sidesaddle. If I sidesaddle this way I slip, I slip in. I am like her in the bed of flowers after her mad lover who had feigned mad, went mad and killed her. He didn't kill her but really he did kill her. You can't go mad and not warn someone. It's an unfair thing to do. Do you think he killed her? they both asked, nodding down their heads, like stable horses might. The Prince? Oh yes. Yes, he killed her. All mad men kill what they love. Often by their killer sulks. Especially by their sulks and their moods. Not in this Bouclé coat, mind. Especially if you're younger than them. If you would only sit in this way keep your feet in here Hun. The heart is leaping outta me watching you straddle that pole. In where? In here. On Dublin. Keep my feet in on Dublin and my legs together sidesaddle? And you've done nothing more than leave me in a Bouclé coat, warm to survive, but not heated enough for us to live. Only to survive. But be in fools. You are not a fool. It will be ok. He survived. You will too. He took a very small fall. I will wake up and I will have this inside my belly. And I can't even find it. But I can't even find it. See. It's not here. Or there. Or anywhere. I can't point it out to you with this index finger. I am blind. There are more ways to be blind than gouging out the eyes. Imagine cutting off the feet. You could. Are you still cold? No. No. Saddle in this way and slip back here. And you can keep the coat. I can? Thank you. Are you ok now? Can you remember the number? Yeah. Ok, let us dial it for you Hun. Call someone to help you. Yes ok. Ok. The Number? 2. 2? Yes 2. I am walking away now. I don't know how else to say it. 2 and me away from you and your kindness. Riddle me this though men of gentle night. How many bottles of gin and herbs would it take now? Would it take for what? A naggin? A shoulder? A baby? A litre? So what volume would it take to divide 2? Divide it in half? No. No, in fact to divide it by 10. Why ten? Because it's not really 2 is it? Not really. A bud is not half a tree if the tree dies, is it? A chick is not half her mother on a plate roasted, is she? A virus can't sustain without the host it kills, a cocoon is only as alive as the butterfly but half and half a cocoon does not make a butterfly winged, my eyes cannot see underwater, my legs cannot run without me. Minus 1 has no potential, has it? Well, yes with a positive. Otherwise, no. I suppose not. But I am not a Siamese twin. Oh awful position, where no one will win. A baby kangaroo in its pouch is not half her mother. The wolf spider's egg sac will be carried by the mother but is not half of her. Ah that's it. Touch the Dublin soil under your feet. Don't mind talking of spiders. Have you drink taken? Or drugs? Lots around here still sniffin' the poppers. Without their coats on. Is the coat warm? It's lovely. Thanks. Mind yourself Hun. Yes boy. Men. I am a woman. And I will try to mind myself on Dublin soil. But you seem to be unaware of my risk. Do you care? This is concrete. Yes, but under it. Think under it, crack it up and destroy it and think of the fertile soil and the earthworms under it. Gouge up the concrete. And then I will see. No. Sadly no. Unless you run the earth through your fingers. But these are weak fingers. They can't fight off anything.

They can sow seeds. Sew buttons.
And so, they are not weak fingers.

And you are warm so you are not weak.

15 | Baksheesh |

You must make sure that they are empty and that they know their crime and give them a scrubbing brush. You must remember the children must not be marked. No one will buy them. Keep the girls alive. Without exerting too much energy. I have a photographer, he is coming later to take pictures, we are thinking of making a brochure of them. A well-educated man, the photographer.

What do you want me for, what do you want with me, do you want anything? I will freeze if you expect anything from me. I am only part of a sequence. I am a Silver Cross pram. I am walking down the street in Athenry. I see my first burka. I am walking and walking and yet I can give you nothing. I am carrying the dead weight in my legs. It haunts my walk.

I am remembering the teenage boys on the
train to Heuston telling me how Molly loved
when one of them would hold her tit
and the other would hold the other tit and
how oh how she said she loved. It. She loved.
It. I asked them did they ask her, Molly, about
what her tits loved, or what she loved
but they said they didn't need to ask her
They knew what Molly liked.

I am a cemetery slab. I am a pine tree. I am a fourteen-year-old unmet dream. I am the wooden owl carver. I am my dead brother's tiny boot. I am a footstep. I am the truck man who hides behind the gate. I am the alter polisher. I am the local doctor. I am scared of the dark. I am the evening lark. I am the cemetery goat. I am choked. I am cold. I am my sister's first host. I am in America. I am always looking for my mother. I am a snooker player. I am gay. I am the eternal day and I am not ok. I am hungry. I am a radio wave. I am tested and depraved. I am my father's wish. I am my mother's dead womb. I am never giving in. I am the identification process. I am the train ticket checker. I am the taxi driver. I am the cot maker. I am the blanket baby knitter. I am the fruit seller. I am the teacher. I am the orchard stealer. I am the dead. I am the child's eyelash flutterer. I am the pissing seven-year-old-stutterer. I am a crown of thorns. I am the goat horn. I am the cook. I am a milkman. I am the van driver. I am a carpenter. I am a fort, a promontory fort.

I am this man's soft navy jumper, riding his steely chest; I lie up against it and beg him to save us.

I am not beyond begging for my sister.
Or my daughter. Or your mother.

I am in my dead Granny's kitchen and she is sweating.
She is making scones. She makes a special gingerbread man for my brother. I give him a bow tie with raisins. It doesn't look too good. Later he flicks off the raisins and chomps down the thing. He never offers me a bite, and I don't like that he has eaten him. It's my secret.

Women need to keep secrets.

This is not my first secret.

Ssshhh they tell us all the time.
Sorry we tell them all the time.

Face to face with the men who would sell the
    world out from under us.

I was always face to face with the men who would sell me.

The world out from under me.

They are a whole alphabet of gestures.

They are a whole language of figurative translation.

Here/There is a pain of woman.
Here/There is a pain of man.

16 | Gavel-Kind |

You're twelve. You have small dark hands and narrow almond hips. You are useful to your father. And your uncle.
You are not sick.

You're forty-two tomorrow. You have lumps all over your chest. You have a high risk of deep-sea swimming to the rock deep bottom today. You are not sick.

You are spread eagled on the green of the college in March. It is Paddy's day. They are taking advantage of the day. And afterwards they steal your red clutch bag with the flick clip. They didn't take advantage of you. You were non advantageous. You are not sick. You are a sign of suffering.

And how bountiful how bountiful how bountiful you are.
Not sick.

You are mothering, you are feeding, lactating. Do you know that bovine mastitis is more researched than human?

You are spreading, don't scream for yourself, now.

How selfish?

Don't feed yourself now.

And that mask over your head, for you to breathe first before you put one on your child? You know that's a head fuck, don't you?

They will judge you in the algae of the Atlantic when your child drowns you know and it will all be your fault.

Always.

You are bated,

oh how bated, how bated how bated you all look, suffering.

17 | Tom Tiddler's Ground, Who Owns a Dead Woman? |

Last Lesson.

How to Put Cake Makeup on a Dying Body.

Last Lesson.

First you wet the blending sponge under the running tap water, you need Prolong Foundation Wear and lots of dry powder as the body stays sweating long after the brain is dead. Really no need for contouring, but up to individual tastes.

> You may hear gas noises
> don't be alarmed

The baby will not coo inside, but it's ok, we'll all hear it coo afterwards.

And what should we do with mum?
 (This is mum with the cherry-cola-lip-stain and the twenty-four-hour-make-up-cake on her face)

Oh mum. Poor mum is dead. So to the morgue. Yes. To the morgue.

But oh what a darling what a darling what a darling she looks.

five

'We never know how high we are
Till we are called to rise;
And then, if we are true to plan,
Our statures touch the skies'

EMILY DICKINSON

Nothing moved until you moved us. And so we
rise. I rise, we rise, don't let a tick betray
us, move the stars, move the clock hands, fly.

Rise

rise out of the ground
                                      rise up out of bed

rouse out of your sleep
                                      wake the dead
                                  arouse the living
wake the feminists   *jaysus don't*   some say let them sleep

                they're only cunts

          wake the nation   burn it steal it fuck it against the wall   dump your boyfriend   he's an asshole

                rise up and be counted

rise up and say – tell me you didn't rise her, tell me you kissed her madly on the lips that you sucked them off her tell me tell me again, blow into my ear

       rise up in a balloon   be a clown

            rise into the station
                                    arouse the nation

   rise up off your head
rise your voice in the gust I can't hear your love
rise your brother tell him you're packing it in
                            rise your mother break her crystal
scatter it on the path   watch it glisten

turn yourself blue   be true   put yourself into
the seawater   surf the waves   rise into them

      ride out of them

rise the red blush on your breasts to your face
    let it out of your head

rise the love in your bed   rise your husband
rise her husband rise your boss   and keep doing it
make them earn it
        make them earn you

  rise them out of it
rise yourself into it

                                       rise the moon
when it fades even if you have to hang it off your prison cell
wall with baling twine

rise your son's interest in Picasso
rise your son's interest in his father
rise up to your envy and shift it

              rise the hay cocks

rise the rowboat on the dock in the grey steel water

           rise the volume on the telly

rise the baby in your belly

rise the bread in the oven and watch it blow
  go   again

rise to the sunrise and scald yourself

rise up your hand and answer my question

rise up your hand and question my question
                      question their question

question your answers   rise up and laugh

throw your head back and fuck them

rise out of your death   rise out of your debt   rise
into your sickness   punch it   punch him

rise another all night   rise your screams
rise behind the bar

arise up out of the bog but bring it with you in the grooves
of your shoes
let some fall from your steps
          leave a trail for your lovers   even in your head

rise your hair and backcomb it   honeycomb it
                    beehive it

                              let them follow you

rise your hand and protest it   rise
your hand   and protect it

          rise a tent and call it home   rise out of
their house let them have it

        rise up out of the sand   but   leave some grains
in your toes

rise out of their shadow   ball it up hock it
back in their direction

     duel with your neighbour   but use a water gun

let go   let fall   rise up and dance

rise up in the wind and let your hair blow

      rise up in the dark and let your mother glow at last

let your father go

fill her out to the shadow of the earth   and sing

rise up and birth them
   rise up and don't birth them
rise your own flags

rise out of their history books and into your history

write it down yourself
                    bring it with you
   even on the back of your hand to remind you

                                it's there, rising.

Notes and Acknowledgements of Influence

Love and thanks unlimited to Aoibheann McCann, Rita Ann Higgins, Heather Higgins-Mackey, Jessie Lendennie, Declan Meade, Katie Raissian, Dani Gill, Elaine Cosgrove, Sarah Clancy, James M Joyce, Des Kenny, Anne Mulhall, Mike McCormack, Mark, Andrea and Catherine Feeney, Saoirse McCann-Callanan and William Wall.

To my poet spouse, Stephen Murray, you're one in a gazillion.

To my real spouse, Ray Glasheen, for the cover again,
and for again and again (and again and again. xxx)

Siobhán Hutson has the patience of a saint. (Or a woman.)

To the book's birth doula, Doireann Ní Ghríofa,
thank you poet-sister.

Finally, thank you friends,
I am more than grateful and more than humbled.

The lines, 'you're dead, do you hear me...' (p.17) from Dave Lordan's "Bullies" (*Invitation to a Sacrifice*, Salmon Poetry, 2010). The lines, '"Show me," I said to our companion....' (p.19) from Seamus Heaney's "A Dream of Jealousy" (*Field Work*, Faber Poetry, 1979). "Journey West" (p32), was inspired by Paul Muldoon in conversation with Nick Laird on Elizabeth Bishop's poem "The Moose" (*The New Yorker*, May 18, 2016). "The Harvest" (p.42) is dedicated to all past residents of The Tuam Mother and Baby Home. "on the nature of things" (p.51) takes its title from Lucretius. "Alternative Truth" (p.54) is inspired by Sarah Clancy's poem, "For the Living and the Dead" (*Thanks for Nothing Hippies*, Salmon Poetry, 2012). "Moderato" (p.58) inspired by the opening movement of Sergei Rachmaninoff's *Piano Concerto No. 2 in C Minor*. "Getting the Priest for Roethke" (p.60) is inspired by Theodore Roethke's time on Inisbofin and Kieran Day's generous retelling of this memory. "Sinéad" (p.61) is dedicated to Sinéad Murray. "I am not a Bog Queen or a Fig or a Pomegranate" (p.66) was written in response to John Montague's foreword in *The Faber Book of Irish Verse* (Faber Poetry, 1974). "and i hope that i don't fall in love with you" (p. 74) takes its title from Tom Waits' song of the same title from the album, *Closing Time* (1973, Asylum Records). "The Banksy Girl" is influenced by the 2002 mural, *Balloon Girl* by graffiti artist, Banksy.

ELAINE FEENEY is an award-winning writer from Galway. *Rise* is her third full poetry collection following *Where's Katie?* (2010) and *The Radio was Gospel* (2014), all published by Salmon. She published her first chapbook, *Indiscipline,* with Maverick Press in 2007. Feeney's work is translated into over a dozen languages and is widely published. In 2016, Liz Roche Company commissioned Feeney to write for a national production to witness and record through dance, film and narrative, the physical experience of being a woman and bodily choice in Ireland. Entitled *Wrongheaded,* a film of the same name, directed by Mary Wycherley, accompanies the production. It premiered at Tiger Dublin Fringe Festival and is currently touring. Feeney has just finished both a pilot comedy series, *The Fannypack*, with writers Aoibheann McCann and Aoife Nic Fhearghusa, which was highly commended by BAFTA, and her first novel, *SIC[K]*. She intends to take a break now and perhaps keep bees or make furniture.

For readings, interviews or review copies contact info@salmonpoetry.com

Tweets @elainefeeney16